WHY SETTLE FOR THE BALCONY?

HOW TO GET A
FRONT-ROW SEAT IN LIFE!

BY MARILYN SHERMAN, CSP

UpFront Presentations
Helping People get a Front-Row seat in life!
www.MarilynSherman.com
e-mail: Marilyn@MarilynSherman.com

Why Settle for the Balcony? How to get a Front-Row Seat in Life

ISBN: 9780966613919

Library of Congress Control Number: 2010910124

Cover design by Dawn Teagarden, Las Vegas Nevada

First Printing August 2005

Printed in the United States of America

LIFE IS SHORT!
LIVE IT IN THE
FRONT-ROW!

I believe everyone deserves a front-row seat in life and I can be the usher to help you get yours!

Other books by Marilyn Sherman, CSP:

- Whose Comfort Zone Are You In?
- Front-Row Service: How to Increase Tip Percentage and Check Average in Your Restaurant
- My Ticket to the Front-Row; A 52-week journal to help you get a front-row seat in life!

About Marilyn Sherman, CSP

Marilyn is known as a Personal Power Expert helping people have more success in their professional and personal lives. She focuses on Visioning, Goal Achievement, and having a No More Excuses mindset.

Since 1993, Marilyn has been motivating and inspiring audiences to get out of their comfort zone and get a front-row seat in life. After starting her career in corporate America, she is now seen as the go-to motivational keynote speaker for corporate and association markets that want their people to improve their morale, increase teamwork, reduce conflict in the workplace and ultimately achieve more results. With her background as a training officer for a major finance company, Marilyn honed her skills to motivate audiences who are often hard to motivate. With her engaging, and fun personality, Marilyn connects with her audiences immediately and delivers content that they can immediately use when they get back to their office.

She has taken her motivational message to conferences, meetings, and conventions in all 50 states, all over Canada and in Bermuda, Mexico, and Germany.

What is a CSP? It is the highest earned designation in the speaking industry called the Certified Speaking Professional. Less than 10% of speakers worldwide have this designation and at the time of this printing Marilyn is only 1 of 181 women worldwide who have this designation.

Marilyn is a graduate of Washington State University. She has served on the boards for the National Speakers Association Las Vegas and San Diego chapters. She also held national positions as the chair of the Motivational Speaker Professional Expert Group. She is married to Yves de Boisredon, The Baron of Wine and lives in Las Vegas, Nevada.

Special Dedication

I would like to dedicate this book to someone who 'gets' it. She understands that a front-row seat is not limited to a first class seat on your favorite airline or a courtside seat at a Los Angeles Lakers game. She understands that being with someone you love, sharing a moment under the stars watching fireworks together is indeed a front-row seat. So, Miss. Haley Schroeder, my beautiful niece, this book is dedicated to you.

Coming Attractions

DIRECTORS' NOTES

Setting the Stage

M̲any people have philosophy about life, but I really like mine. I call it a "Front-Row Philosophy"™. You see, I believe that life is lived in the front-row. I love to sit in the front-row of seminars, conferences, concerts, sporting events, and even church! The only place I don't like sitting up front would be at the movie theater or at a Blue Man show in Las Vegas. Other than that, I love being in the front-row.

The more I experienced being in the front-row, the more I began to see the parallels of life and a venue for a big event. Depending on the venue and the event, sections have names. There is the *mezzanine, orchestra, upper balcony*, and even *view obstructed*. However, for the purposes of this book, I will narrow down the venue seating into three areas. **The Front-Row** (VIP section where front-row seats are – usually right down in front and center), **General Admission** (where most people sit) and, finally, the **Balcony** (when you're on a budget or you buy tickets at the last minute and you're forced to sit in the view obstructed seats at the top (otherwise known as the 'nose-bleed' section).

The funny thing about looking at life this way is that we have seats all over the place. If we are in the top physical shape of our lives, then we have our 'physical seat' in the front-row. If we are lacking ambition with our work and simply do the very minimum to get by, then our 'work seat' is in general admission. If your spirit is broken down because of an inappropriate or abusive relationship, and you have very little hope for your future, you are stuck in the balcony with your relationship seat. Therefore, you can be sitting in different sections at the same time. It just depends on what part of your life you happen to be examining.

My goal is simple. I want to inspire you to look at where you are sitting now and take your balcony and general admission seats and move them closer to the front-row. Don't complain. Don't wallow in guilt. Don't even live in the seat of regret. And, whatever you do, don't start comparing your seat to where others sit and make up stories as to how they got there. You see, sometimes when people aren't happy with where they are in life, they look at other people who have what they want. Then, if they don't have healthy self-esteem and confidence, they make up why the others 'have it so good' and then complain why they can't have the same breaks in life. Here's my suggestion – if you see someone who has what you want, a job, a title, a great relationship, a great physical body, whatever it is that someone has that you want, approach them and mention your admiration or respect for what they have or what they have done, and then ask if they could give you advice. "What would you say to someone like me, who wants a job like yours?" for example. Chances are, if you come from a place of admiration and a sincere desire to learn, they will help you.

Take a look at where your seats are and move up.

Take some steps to make every seat you sit in, a front-row seat. I want you to be, from now on, a front-row person! In fact, after reading this book, hopefully you will be inspired to be a front-row person too. To help you know what that looks like, chapter one describes what front-row people are like.

There are twelve chapters in this book – or scenes rather, to go with the ol' theater theme. In each scene, you will be offered strategies, suggestions, and examples of how to get a front-row seat in life. As an added bonus, I've added 'Front-Row' stories from some of my friends and colleagues. It's always interesting to learn what others interpretation is of a front-row seat.

You deserve a front-row seat in life and I want to help you get there. I offer you 7 strategies – actually 6 strategies of what to do, and one strategy of what NOT to do – that will help you change your life for the positive.

I am inspired that you are reading this. By reading the stories, and by following the examples, and suggestions in this book, you too will be sitting in the front-row of your own life. My hope for you is that you have fun along the journey to YOUR front-row and once you get there, I hope you enjoy the view!*

   - Marilyn Sherman, CSP

* If you are interested in the accompanying journal for this book titled *"My Ticket to the Front-Row – A 52 week journal with inspirational thoughts to guide you to the Front-Row"*, or the CD of Marilyn's live keynote presentation on getting a front-row seat in life, please go to

LIFE IS SHORT!

SCENE ONE

WHO'S DOWN IN FRONT?

What's a *Front-Row* Person?

If life is a venue, and the best seats in the house are reserved for 'front-row' people, then who are they? What makes them so special to be sitting in the V.I.P. section?

Actually, they are not particularly special at all. They do seem to have common traits that make them worthy of the label 'front-row' person. It is safe to say that the one thing front-row people have in common is that they are constantly striving to be better. Of course, they have the capacity to enjoy their successes and take in the view, but they aren't complacent. I have come up with a list of 52 traits that front-row people strive to have. As you read this book and if you are journaling your successes, keep in mind this list of traits. You too can adapt and adopt these traits as well. You ultimately determine if you are a Front-Row person. Having traits that are common to successful front-row people would be a great start.

By the way, these 52 traits are the same traits in the journal 'My Ticket to the Front-Row.' I wanted you to have one trait a week that you could think about, focus on, and take some action on, so after one year, you'll be well into the habit of being a front-row person!

Traits Of Front-Row People

Here's a list of what front-row people are like. They:

- strive for excellence
- strive to acknowledge their wrongdoings
- strive to be a valuable friend
- strive to be accountable for their success or failures
- strive to be ambitious
- strive to be appreciative
- strive to be bighearted
- strive to be charitable
- strive to be courageous
- strive to be creative
- strive to be dedicated
- strive to be diligent
- strive to be down to earth
- strive to be free of negativity
- invest in their personal development
- invest in their professional development
- love to read
- plan on a bright future
- share their success
- strive to be generous
- strive to be happy

- strive to be helpful

- strive to be hopeful

- strive to be inspiring

- strive to be level-headed

- strive to be motivated

- strive to be of service

- strive to be open minded

- strive to be productive

- strive to be reliable

- strive to be resilient

- strive to be studious

- strive to be true to themselves

- strive to be trustworthy

- strive to be visionaries

- strive to celebrate accomplishments

- strive to enjoy life

- strive to follow-through with commitments

- strive to act in alignment with their value system

- strive to forgive

- strive to give and live abundantly

- strive to learn new things

- strive to let go of resentments

- strive to live in the moment
- strive to live with integrity
- strive to love themselves more
- strive to never give up
- strive to step up to a challenge
- strive to surround themselves with positive people
- strive to take calculated risks
- study people of substance
- feel worthy of a Front-Row Seat!

Wow – what a list. My intention is that you look at this list and see the beginning of a roadmap for yourself. Don't be discouraged. Many people say 'I don't know where to begin. I don't even know what a front-row seat would be for me.' If that is the case for you, relax. Re-read the list of 52 traits with the words "Do I….?" in front of each trait. If there are areas that are a definite "NO" for you, make a goal for yourself to be more like that.

Have fun with it, be courageous with it. Embrace it.

Your Front-Row is waiting to be created!

SCENE TWO

THE BALCONY
IN THE
BEGINNING

The First Balcony

Have you ever had an experience in your life that if you were to categorize it, you would say it was definitely a balcony seat experience? You know, a time where you felt like an outsider, unworthy of sitting in the front-row? When I started speaking on this topic, I went to a speech coach to help me with my keynote of the same title as this book. My friend Susan Clarke posed this question to me:

"So Marilyn, what about you? When have you ever had a balcony experience?"

I didn't have to think very long to recall an experience that I will never forget. Dr. Phil would call this a 'defining moment' in my life. This particular event happened when I was in the 7th grade. To give you a bit of a background, all growing up I was considered a 'jock'. Sports were all I really aspired to do and do well. As an athletic pre-teen with a nickname of 'Moose', the only play I had with the boys usually involved a field, court, or a tetherball. I had really pretty girlfriends that the boys would flirt with, but not me, I was their rival in all things athletic.

Being a jock however, did not prevent me from having a crush on the best-looking boy in our class. We used to say he was 'such a fox'!

One day, he surprised me and asked me to go to the park and 'make out' with him (I don't know what they call it today, but back then it meant heavy kissing).

I got all nervous because I couldn't believe he was asking *me*. Did he just choose me out of all of my girlfriends? Alison, Julie, Robin, Kim, and Meg were all so much cuter than me and so much more popular with the boys than me.

But, he said, there was a catch. He wanted me to meet him behind Island Park Elementary School.... at midnight!

I thought to myself, he wants me to sneak out of my house in the middle of the night, walk to Island Park all by myself, just to meet him and make out? After about 2 seconds of hesitation, I gave him my answer.

"Okay."

I know this incident happened over 35 years ago, so the details of the event are a bit cloudy, naturally. But, one thing happened that was crystallized in my head that I'll never forget. It's what he said to me when we were done with our little kissing session.

He said, "Don't tell anyone."

I was devastated. I immediately felt hurt and unworthy to be seen with in public. Now, I'm certainly not going to blame all of my failed relationships on this one incident. But, it did have an effect on me and my self-image at the time. And, it was my first real memory of a balcony experience. As an adult, I have learned that when I act arrogant, or cocky, it's because my fear and insecurity is raising its ugly head. And the fear and insecurity that luckily has waned dramatically since my youth, stems from this very incident. I'll talk more about the dangers of being cocky in Scene 10 on 'What NOT to do'.

Now that you know one of my balcony experiences, can you think of one for yourself? Maybe it's a bad relationship, maybe it's a job you took that was degrading, or maybe it's a situation that you were in that didn't honor you. Think about it for a minute. Think about how the balcony seat is not a choice seat to be in. Think of how secretly unhappy you were then, and how you never want to return to the balcony again.

Now it's time to relax, release and renew yourself! Read this book with an open mind and start to look at all the seats in your life. Pretty soon you will be asking yourself "Is this a front-row seat for me?" If not, you will have the tools to re-arrange the seating in your life to move up to the front-row!

Balcony Seat Examples:

1. You're in a dead-end job that is so over-the-top stressful that you can't even remember what you liked about this job.

2. You're in a relationship that is not rewarding, or not safe, or not comforting, but you stay because you're 'so in love' or you're too afraid to be alone.

3. You've let your physical body go to the point where you're too embarrassed to go out and do fun things like dance, attend bar-b-que's, or go swimming with friends. Just thinking about such social events leads you to turn to unhealthy habits of becoming

one with your couch eating your favorite binge food.

4. You are so obsessed with impressing people; you end up buying exorbitant gifts, constantly picking up dinner tabs, offering to do things for people knowing they won't really appreciate it. Every time you feel taken advantage of, you realize that you have this fear that people won't like you unless you are giving something to them. This fear of not having any friends has resulted in you creating a circle of artificial friends.

FRONT-ROW STORY

Marilyn, I wanted to drop a note as I was writing in my journal about being in the front row at work . . .

I want to be at a better show.

I mean, I am putting forth my best effort here. My job is, as Jerry MaGuire said "an up at dawn, pride-swallowing journey that I will NEVER fully tell you about." And I do it. And I'm great at it. Nobody (No Body) can turn a hot customer around like me. However, THIS is not the concert I want to be at. I feel like I'm at the Barney show but I'm all dressed up for Tina Turner or Santana (Santana fans!).

Anyways, that's it. Just the need to be at a better show. I'm in the front row here: I'm just seeing Barney. "I love you. You love me." . . . When it could be a little racier!

Name withheld .... until she gets a front-row seat!

SCENE THREE

GENERAL
ADMISSION

Everyone at one point has probably been to an event where his or her ticket stub read "General Admission." It doesn't mean the seat is necessarily bad, but it could be better. Just like some seats people are living in right now. Here's what they say sometimes when they are rationalizing being where they are:

"I don't love my job, but I don't hate it either. Hey at least I have a job."

"My boyfriend's not bad. He's certainly not Mr. Right, but he's Mr. Right Now. Besides, it's nice to have him around while I'm waiting for something better to come along."

"I know I haven't worked out in awhile, and I need to actually use my gym membership for it to work, but at least I'm not like that huge guy in accounting."

"Of course I'm not happy with what I do. But, in just 7 short years, I can retire!"

The late James Newman coined the term 'comfort zone' and did some extensive writing and speaking on the subject. Many years later, I wrote a book not just about the dangers in staying in your comfort zone, but also the danger of jumping into someone else's. Your comfort zone is a safe comfortable place that even though it's not ideal, it's familiar to you and it's very tempting to remain there.

People live and work in their comfort zone for several reasons. It's safe, it's secure, it's familiar, and it's what they know. However, I would hate to go through my entire life being safe. The late Rear Admiral Grace Murray Hopper (and the inventor of the CoBAL computer system) said, "A Ship in port is safe...but that's not what ships are built for."

If you want to be truly happy and successful, you must take some risks along the way. Once you realize that your comfort zone will eventually turn into a rut, you are more likely to make some sort of changes, hopefully for the better. That's when you have to be careful not to jump out of your comfort zone and make decisions because other people are telling you or pressuring you to do it.

I wrote my first book "Whose Comfort Zone Are You In?" * after realizing that I was listening to other people about how to live my life. In a nutshell, I was living in Allentown, Pennsylvania working for Chrysler First Financial Services. My ultimate dream was to become a motivational speaker and my job as a trainer in Human Resources was a good stepping stone position.

When the time came to interview for a seminar company my dad was concerned that I was leaving a stable, safe environment. My dream meant that I would leave that steady paycheck and become an independent contractor speaking full time.

His exact words were:

> "You're making good money, you have a good job and Chrysler is not going anywhere. So, why don't you stay in Allentown?"
>
> I listened long enough to finish the call with "Hey Dad, thanks

for sharing."

I did leave my job in Allentown, packed up all of my belongings and moved to San Diego. It was risky, but I loved fulfilling my dream of traveling around the country speaking full time. Ironically, that division of Chrysler was sold to NationsBank and all 450 of my colleagues in Allentown had to relocate out of state or find another job. If I would have stayed in Allentown because my dad said I had a 'good job', not only would I have been living in my dad's comfort zone, but it would have been a general admission seat for sure.

I know a lot of people who would have loved to have that job and have a steady paycheck with good benefits. And, I certainly would have made the best of it. But, I would have always longed to be a speaker and had I not taken the chance to go out on my own, I may have blamed my dad for giving me bad advice. I believe that's how seeds of anger and resentment are planted in people. When you listen to other people say what you should do with your life, your career, your goals, they sometimes do not have your best interest in mind. Sometimes out of their own fears or their own insecurities, they project that fear into you and suggest you stay where you are.

I remember having a conversation with my friend Jana Stanfield. She is an accomplished singer/songwriter living in Nashville. I was telling her how I wanted to leave a job that was really comfortable, but not my front-row job. She asked me a question that really made a difference for me. She said: "You're staying in someone else's dream job. How long are you going to keep it from them?" I thought that was a really interesting take on my situation. Jana and her partner Jimmy Scott wrote a fantastic song called "If I Were Brave." I believe that if more people were brave, they would leave their general admission situations (or, worse, their balcony situations) and they would go out and get their front-row seat.

Their lyrics include:

What would I do if I knew that I could not fail? If I believed would the wind always fill up my sail? How far would I go, what could I achieve, trusting the hero in me?

If I were brave I'd walk the razor's edge, where fools and dreamers dare to tread. Never lose faith, even when losing my way, what step would I take today if I were brave?

What if we're all meant to do what we secretly dream? What would you ask if you knew you could have anything? Like the mighty oak sleeps in the heart of a seed, are there miracles in you and me?

This is a great song. I recommend getting a copy of her CD and listening to it every day. And, if you don't want to listen to her CD, at least do yourself a favor, and ask yourself 3 times a day "What would I do today if I were brave?" This question will change the way you make decisions! Be brave! Get out of your balcony or general admission seat by getting out of your comfort zone!

Some people say they have no problem living in their comfort zone, or their 'general admission' seat. That's fine. In fact, they probably wouldn't even have bothered to pick up this book! My message is for people who have a burning desire to do more, be more, have more and give more. Maybe you don't have a burning desire to have all of the above, but maybe you have one or two of your seats in general admission or the balcony. Things aren't bad, they're not great, they are just average. Then, this book is for you.

I remember speaking to the Club Managers Association of America about how to get out of a rut, how to change your perspective and make any seat a front-row seat. Not long after this convention, I got an e-mail from an attendee who went home and discussed my topic with his wife.

"Honey, we're living in the front-row, aren't we?"

They talked about their life, their relationship and decided that in fact they had been playing it safe...too safe for them. It sounded to me like their relationship had moved smoothly right into a comfort zone. Sure they had a good marriage, good jobs, but they hadn't taken a fun adventurous vacation in a long time. So they asked themselves 'What would front-row people do?'. They had fun thinking of the possibilities, and not long after that conversation, an opportunity came along to go on a 10 day Alaskan cruise, and they jumped on it! For them, a cruise was a front-row seat! They were so happy that the following year they booked their second one. They are out of their general admission now and are living in the front-row!

What comfort zone would you leave if you were brave?

_____

_____

_____

_____

Tim Gard's front-row story

As an experienced road warrior who travels over 150,000 miles each year from Texas to Tasmania and Fargo to Fiji, I have to work very hard to have fun as I fly or I'll burn out and not be able to do my work anymore.

My favorite seat on any airplane is in the front-row, IN FIRST CLASS! I don't like to pay for first class so part of the fun challenge for me every trip is to see if I can get upgraded to first class for free when I check in at the ticket counter. I discovered very quickly that simply asking: "Can you upgrade me for free?" is usually met with the reply: "Why should I upgrade you?" and then my reply would often fall short of securing the coveted front row bulkhead first class seat when I would simply answer: "Because I like first class, I like it a lot."

I discovered it required a better, more original effort on my part to secure my front-row dream seat, failure is not an option. Now when the gate agent says: "Why should I upgrade you?" I answer: "Because if you don't I'll hold my breath until you upgrade me!" I then inhale deeply, noisily and hold my breath and slowly turn from red then blue. Usually the gate agent will nervously laugh then see I mean business and begin to check first class availability and then start to laugh.

It does not work all the time, but it has worked. It actually works best when I am in a really nice suit, they look and see I am a 100,000 mile a year customer, a million miler flyer and yet I still enjoy flying and having fun. Then they do what they can to accommodate me. P.S. If you try it, remember to not hold your breath till you pass out. Important safely tip here. FYI.

– Tim Gard, CSP www.timgard.com
Denver, Colorado

SCENE FOUR
FRONT-ROW BABY!

h, the front-row. Nirvana. Best seat in the house! This seat
represents that moment when you look around and say: "It
doesn't get any better than this!"

When I ask people to share with me their favorite front-row story, it
amazes me to see how different people's views are. Some people
take me very literally, others figuratively. Take my niece Emily for
example. She wrote about her favorite thing to do and at first it looks
like she's talking about her friends going to these shows where local
bands play. But after reading it again, it was really quite philosophical.

FRONT-SEAT AT GRACELAND

At least once a month, my friends and I try to catch
a show. One of our favorite spots is Graceland, smack
in the heart of downtown Seattle. This place is as big
as my backyard and it's always PACKED full of
people. There is so little room that it's crazy. You
make friends almost instantly. The first thing we do
when we get there is try to get to the front. The front
is like, the best, you're up close, you can grab the
band, and you are almost safe from all the crowd
surfers. Once you get there, you're home free, you've
made it. Now you can enjoy the show. We never get
there right away, it takes work, we have to nudge and
budge our way, we clash with others who are looking

for the same spot, sometimes it takes all night to get there, but as long as we get there for the last band, we're usually happy. On the way to the front, you meet people, you share your thoughts on the upcoming sets, you find out peoples' life stories and share your own, and it's great. Getting to the front is everyone's goal; it's the best seat in the house, we all want it, but it certainly isn't long enough. When we get there, we have won; we have shown our dedication to the band, we've passed all the weak people who obviously don't share the same passion for our music. It's just the best place to be, I can't even enlighten you with all of my knowledge, I mean, something needs to be left for the reader to find out themselves right? Get out there, find a show, and get to the front, you'll see what I mean; you'll never want to leave.

– Emily Cook, Age 15, Seattle, Washington

I love Emily's energy. She really gets it. I love how she says that it's not easy, and it does take time. Isn't that how life is? You have to nudge and budge and eventually you get there. I also like how she mentioned meeting people on the way to the front-row and finding out about their stories as you share your own. This is my front-row philosophy in a nutshell!

She's pretty insightful at 15 – my guess is she'll have no problem living in the front-row!

My husband and I have incorporated this philosophy into our every day language. Before we were married, Yves and I went to Puerto Vallarta to visit his cousin Peter and his wife Bea. We had a wonderful time and at one point, all of us were lounging on lawn chairs at a secluded beach at the Presidente Hotel. Peter asked us all what we were reading. We had novels, trashy magazines, and mysteries. He looked at us and said:

"Look....look at the waves, the ocean, the sky....it doesn't get any better than this!"

Certainly, sitting on a beach watching waves and sand crabs would qualify for a front-row seat. But, Yves surprised me even more later that evening.

He arranged a 'date night' for just the two of us at one of Peter and Bea's favorite restaurants in Puerto Vallarta called "La Palapa". It was the most romantic, awe-inspiring dinners I have ever experienced. Not only did Yves choose the menu ahead of time, but when we arrived at our scheduled reservation time, we knew we were living in the front-row.

La Palapa is a wonderful open-air restaurant right on the beach. There are booths and tables that fill the restaurant, all tiered to take advantage of the beautiful ocean view. There were even plenty of tables right on the beach.

I noticed a path of lanterns in the sand leading from the main restaurant to two beautifully set tables right at the edge of the ocean. There were candles, flowers, tiki torches; and the guided walkway reminded me of a landing strip. The host led us right down that path and invited us to take our seats at the table that was fully set for dinner for two. Our drink orders were taken and our waiter asked us what time we would like our dinner to be served. Then at that designated time, one course after another was brought to our exclusive, one-of-a-kind table on the beach!

It was magnificent. After a scrumptious meal, we were invited to the second table for our after-dinner drinks. I mentioned to the waiter that I had taken my sandals off under the table and I needed to put them on before moving. He gently said "no worries, that is your table for the night. You can leave them there as long as you like!"

It wasn't long after we moved to our 2nd table that fireworks went off in the sky above. It truly was a front-row experience that was all the more special because Yves had planned the whole thing and surprised me with it.

A front-row seat can be just that, a seat in the front, exclusive from all the seats behind. However, it doesn't have to be that literal.

If you are feeling special, you are in a front-row seat.

If you love what you do, and you are doing what you love, you are in a front-row seat.

If you are in love, and that love is reciprocated, you are in a front-row seat.

If you have a friend that you can call on, and they can count on you when they need you, you are in a front-row seat.

If you recognize that you have a talent and you use it to help others, you are in a front-row seat.

If you realize that you are a special individual and that you are loved unconditionally, then you are in a front-row seat.

GETTING YOUR OWN FRONT-ROW

So what does your front-row look like? It could be a show, it could be the birth of an infant, it could be a connection with someone. It can be a place, a specific chair, but it doesn't have to be. A front-row seat is anywhere that you determine is your front-row seat. Here are some more examples:

Nido Qubein, Chairman of Great Harvest Bread company and president of High Point University - winning the Horatio Alger Award for distinguished Americans

Carin Stutz, Past president of Cosi Restaurants – speaking to a group of girls while on a trip to a third-world country about how they could grow up and be executives or even the president of company

Tim Dietzler, Director Dining Services at Villanova University – winning an acting contest as a teen for his one-man show.

Jack Canfield, Speaker/best-selling author – Sitting courtside at the NBA finals watching the Chicago Bulls with friends – all wearing for the TV cameras t-shirts that spelled out "Chicken" "Soup" "For The" "Soul" (Maybe that's how they went on to sell over 100 million copies of their books!).

Jay Marshall, Executive Chef – watching the 1989 world series in San Francisco when the earth quake hit!

You see, your front-row seat is totally up to you – what makes you feel like 'It doesn't get any better than this!'

So how do you do it? How do you move up and sit, live and have moments, in the front-row? First, define for yourself what a front-row seat is. What does a front-row look like to you? What is the first thing that comes to your mind? Once you've determined your ultimate front-row seat, than you can analyze where you are currently seated and go from there. Look bigger – see bigger – open your mind to bigger possibilities instead of the limited vision most of us are used to.

MISSY MAIO'S FRONT-ROW SEAT

Marilyn, you were great! Jessica and I stumbled the first day into the workshop you were covering by accident. Not only did we have a great time, but immediately following your talk, we had a great experience.

After leaving your seminar at the Women's Foodservice Forum, pumped up and ready to "get into the front-row," my work associate Jessica and myself walked out of the convention hall and noticed big red signs with arrows pointing to a late afternoon poolside event. This event wasn't in our handy convention guide, but we followed the signs out to the pool, where upon noticing frozen cosmopolitans, we made a quick decision to go 'straight to the front-row!' We approached the table, big smiles and very confident, received our "light up" Cosmo glasses, beads for around our necks, and proceeded into the invitation only party. We drank a few cocktails and then were personally invited over to the cabanas for a 10 minute massage. What a great experience directly following your seminar of "Why Settle for the Balcony? How to get a Front Row Seat in Life!" We had a blast! Thanks for you energy and overall great attitude you have! You are a constant reminder of how fabulous life can be if you are doing exactly what you enjoy doing!

– Missy Maio, New Jersey

SCENE FIVE

YOUR TICKET PLEASE

"…SO, WHERE'S YOUR SEAT?"

Assessment Time

L et's take a look at where you are in your life right now. This simple self-assessment is meant for you to see where you think you are right now in terms of balcony, general admission and front-row. Once you take the assessment, you can then determine where you would like to put your effort and energy to move up to the front-row.

If you were to look at your life as a venue, where is your seat in each of these areas? Remember, there are no right or wrong answers here. Just indicate where you think you are right now.

Directions:

Go down the list of each area of your life, and put a check mark in the box that would best describe where that seat is for you. There are no right or wrong answers, this is just meant to raise your awareness of where you are right now.

Area:	Balcony (Bad view, not ideal, but at least you're there)	General Admission (Not bad, not great, comfort zone setting in)	Front-Row! It doesn't get any better than this!
Your Work	❑	❑	❑
Your health	❑	❑	❑
Your friendships	❑	❑	❑
Your personal relationship	❑	❑	❑
Your Faith	❑	❑	❑
Your Attitude	❑	❑	❑

Lets take a closer look at each of the different areas that are on the self-assessment.

YOUR WORK

How are you doing with your work? Whether you own your own business or you work for someone else. How are you doing? Are you enthusiastic, creative, and confident in what you do? Do feel pride in your work so much that you would welcome an audit from your boss or best customer to see how well you do? If so, then your work is definitely front-row work. To love what you do and to get paid for it is truly a blessing. I heard that the only time someone is truly happy and enthusiastic about their work is when it's their first week on the job or their last week on the job! Seriously, I have met many people who have lost their enthusiasm for their work. They have forgotten what they love about their craft because they have been sidetracked in one way or another.

I know people who clearly articulate that they don't like their job, but they are making a decent salary and with that comfort of a steady paycheck they can dedicate their free time to doing a hobby that they love. Others don't know how they got into such a rut, but if they were courageous, they would leave. But, knowing the job market, and knowing the competition, they fall back in their comfort zone and stay...counting down the days to the weekend or worse, their retirement.

YOUR HEALTH

How is your health? This would encompass all things that have do with your mental and physical health. Look at your habits. How are they? Focus on all of your habits that effect your health. For example, your sleeping habits, eating habits, smoking, and exercise. Also, talk a look at your social habits like setting boundaries to prevent overwhelm, saying yes when you really wanted to say no, or holding in your thoughts, feelings, opinions because you don't feel worthy of speaking up.

The thing about your health is that it affects all other things. My great uncle John McPherson worked very hard in his life building a company from the ground up. He bought an association when it was floundering and turned it into a corporation. With 10 people, they delivered flowers from growers to the market and with the help of family and a clearly defined vision; he grew that company to be a world leader in freight forwarding called Airborne Freight Corporation. The common name was Airborne Express. In 2004, Airborne was acquired by DHL for $1.5 billion. It took a lot of dedication, hard work, and sacrifice to build such a company. Unfortunately, by the time he decided to step down as CEO and spend more time enjoying the fruits of his labor, he had cancer. I realized that I would no longer get to enjoy riding his horses on his ranch in Marin County or playing tennis with him and just hanging out with him. Luckily, we were able to do those things while he was healthy. However, many people never take the time to enjoy front-row experiences with their family and friends, because they have work to do. Just don't wait until it's too late. My dad has semi-retired, but at 84 years old, he hasn't slowed down much. Recently I was able to share a front-row moment with him. His hobby is collecting and showing classic cars. He's a Ford guy, so he has amassed a nice Ford collection. The one he was showing recently when I came to visit him was his 1965 convertible baby blue Thunderbird. The show was near the Texas Motor Speedway and what fun it was to have all the classic thunderbirds in the show drive over in single file, line up and drive around the track 10 at a time! He was really in his glory, wearing his baseball cap backwards and showing off his classic car. What joy it was for me to see him in his front-row seat!

My mom recently came with me to a speaking engagement in San Jose. After my keynote, there was an event at a museum that was totally catered by the Stanford University foodservices department. She was so full of joy tasting all these wonderful foods and having people from my audience come up to her saying 'Hi Mom!'. I had to take a picture of her because she was having so much fun enjoying the moment!

I agree with W.M. Lewis who said, "The tragedy of life is not that it ends so soon, but that we wait so long to begin it."

YOUR FRIENDSHIPS

Friends are blessings for sure. True friends are those people that no matter how long time goes by between coffee dates, or phone calls, the very next time you connect with them, it seems like yesterday. Do you have front-row friends? If you have one, you are truly blessed. One thing I like to tell my audiences is to connect with your best friend, and let them know that of all the people in the world, they are your front-row best friend. Friends move, they get sick, they lose touch, and it can be very painful. But, who said you can't get new friends? Be open to new friendships and relationships and your life can be enriched unexpectedly!

I remember speaking for the first time at the Women's Foodservice Forum in Orlando and met some terrific leaders in the foodservice industry. They have since been one of my best clients, hiring me for the last 10 years in a row and counting. They are an amazing, dynamic group of leaders. One woman, Erika Von Heiland, in particular was so energetic after my talk that we exchanged cards so we could keep in touch. She was inspired by my talk as much as I was inspired by the fact that she was a two-time Olympic athlete. After getting to know each other a little bit, she told me her best friend lived in Las Vegas and we just have to meet! Not only did I meet with her friend Lori Wilkinson, but Erika recently visited Las Vegas and we all got together for a great dinner and a show at the Bellagio. We had a blast! Although Erika and Lori are new friends, they are front-row friends for sure. In fact Yves and I recently went to a convention in Atlanta and Erika hosted us for dinner and we even stayed at her home for one night! Both Erika and Lori came to San Francisco for my wedding and helped me get ready for my big day. And, every July 22, Lori and her husband Glenn and Yves and I find a way to celebrate my birthday in style. I cherish their friendships more than I can express here.

There are a lot of Erika's and Lori's out there. If you are feeling stuck with your friendships, or you have noticed that there are some people who just don't 'fill your bucket' with good stuff, then it's not too late to find new friends.

Ever since I started speaking on this subject of living life in the front-row, I have received the following poem. Every time I get it, it is attached with 'author unknown'. I have done some research and I still can't identify who wrote it. Nevertheless, it is fantastic and it fits so well with the theme of this book and in particular this chapter. If you know who the original author was, please forward that information to me, so I can give proper credit in future publications.

THE FRONT ROW

Life is a Theater....Invite Your Audience Carefully.

Not everyone is healthy enough to have a front row seat in our lives.

There are some people in your life that need to be loved from a DISTANCE.

It's amazing what you can accomplish when you let go of or at least minimize your time with draining, negative, incompatible, not going anywhere relationships or friendships.

Observe the relationships around you. Pay close attention. Which ones lift and which ones lean? Which ones encourage and which ones discourage?

Which ones are on a path of growth uphill and which ones are going downhill?

When you leave certain people, do you feel better or feel worse?

Which ones always have drama or don't really understand, know or appreciate you?

The more you see quality, respect, growth, peace of mind, love and truth around you....the easier it will become for you to decide who gets to sit in the front row and who should be moved to the balcony of your life.

Remember that the people we hang with will have an impact on both of our lives and our income.

And so, we must be careful to choose the people we hang out with, as well as the information with which we feed our minds. We can't change who is around us, but we can choose we are around.

We should not share our dreams with negative people, nor feed them with negative thoughts.

Who's in your front row?

-Author unknown

The late motivational speaker and accomplished businessman Jim Rohn said; "You are the average of the five people you spend the most time with." So look around and ask if you need to spend more time with people that inspire you, motivate you, challenge you to be a better you.

YOUR PERSONAL RELATIONSHIP

Everyone deserves to be treated with respect. Sometimes we get so caught up with love, infatuation, even lust that we make poor judgment decisions when it comes to relationships, and we don't even realize the disrespectful behavior of our 'significant' other. Sometimes we even realize the person we are engaged to is the wrong person, but because the invitations have been mailed and the deposit on the catering services has been paid, that we don't have the courage to call the whole thing off.

My wish for you is this: If you have a companion in your life, I wish that they are healthy and that they treat you with the utmost respect and unconditional love. If not, please know that you deserve that. I have been in my share of balcony relationships where I convinced myself that if I waited long enough, he would 'change'. Ha! Once I saw the truth in my own balcony situation, I settled for general admission. I figured, why not have fun while I'm waiting for the front-row guy to appear! Then, I realized, I had a front-row person right in front of me! Now I really know what respect is in a relationship. It's wonderful! This is the first time in my life that I have a front-row personal relationship and it feels really good.

Sure, there are people that say they don't need someone in order to be happy and fulfilled. That's great! I just know for me, I really wanted a family, and someone to share my life with and I deserve that person to be a good person with a good heart. My husband, Yves, is that person and he constantly shows me front-row seats. I am very blessed that he chose to be with me on this journey to the front-row.

YOUR FAITH

How is your faith? Do you see light at the end of the proverbial tunnel? Do you see good in people, situations, and circumstances? Faith is a positive expectation of any circumstances' outcome.

Faith is doing the right thing even when no one is watching. Faith is having integrity. We make thousands of decisions every day and having faith helps us make the right decisions for the right reasons.

Where is your faith? Are you stuck in the balcony seething in contempt? Or are you meandering around in general admission not knowing what your purpose is, and you're waiting for some sort of sign? Or, do you have front-row faith? Of course, that's open to personal interpretation. One friend describes front-row faith as knowing that God loves you totally and unconditionally. Faith is the absence of discouragement, fear and hatred. Where's your faith chair?

Zig Ziglar has been an influential speaker in my industry and a man who really inspired me when I was growing up. Thankfully, I have had the opportunity to see him at conventions and conferences and one time I was able to sit with him over lunch and ask him, "Out of all of the life experiences that you've had, what is one of your favorite front-row seats where you said 'it doesn't get any better than this'. Can you think of one?" Without hesitation, he said it was a trip he took with his wife to Jerusalem. They were in a church and he looked at her and saw that she was more beautiful that day than the day he had married her some 30 years earlier. He said he felt a bit guilty because she was beautiful the day they married. Then, it hit him. He was looking at her as if she were already forgiven, and it changed the way he saw her. Wow. That was strong. But your faith can be demonstrated in many ways that don't include church.

One of my favorite stories that I like to tell in my speeches is about a fifth grader named Lin Hao. He was the 9-year boy who walked in the opening ceremonies of the 2008 Summer Olympics in Beijing China with basketball great Yao Ming. The reason why he had the prestigious honor of walking in the stadium in front of millions of viewers around the world is because he was a survivor in an earthquake that devastated his elementary school. Once he got out alive, he went back in and saved two of his classmates who were unconscious. I also read that he led his classmates in song to keep their spirits up while waiting for rescuers. When he was finally rescued, they asked him why he went back into the rubble to save his classmates and he responded;

"It was my job. I'm the hall monitor."

Isn't that the cutest thing? This 9-year boy showed strength, integrity, and quickness in action to help others. That to me is a manifestation of faith.

ATTITUDE

Finally, how's your attitude? Are you filled with gratitude and give people the benefit of the doubt? Do you see the bright side of situations? Or are you like some people who are such a drag that they brighten up a room just by leaving it? That would be balcony attitude for sure. Your attitude is worth so much. I have often heard Human Resource directors say they would rather hire someone for their attitude and train for skill instead of the other way around. I believe one of the reasons Southwest Airlines is so successful is because they hire people with fun, outrageous attitudes! I was on a Southwest flight just last night and the flight attendant spiced up the safety instructions by saying "In the event of loss of air cabin pressure, put your oxygen mask on first, then help the child next to you if you have one. If you have more than one child next to you, decide now which one is your favorite!" She had a sense of humor for sure. The funny thing is, people that would usually tune out to the safety instructions were listening intently. After she was done, she actually got a round of applause!

I also learned a simple lesson from my friend Steve Kime. I saw him doing an exercise during a staff training session and I want to share it with you now. He asked the audience to look at the 26 letters of the alphabet. Each letter represents a value from 1 to 26, with A = 1 and Z = 26 for example. He then wrote the word ATTITUDE on a flip chart and put the value next to each letter, and showed what happened when you added the totals up. They add up to 100.

Your Attitude is so important. It sounds like it would be so obvious, but people often forget. Sales people know that customers want to buy from people who have a good attitude, employees want to work harder for bosses who have a good attitude, it's human nature to be naturally drawn to people with good attitudes. Just look at the restaurant industry. People are more likely to leave better tips and return to an establishment if the food server has a good attitude. I was dining recently at a nice seafood restaurant where our waiter was really cocky. He was robotic in his delivery of the menu and the specials, and then interrupted our conversation when he delivered the food. My guests' food wasn't cooked right, and he ignored her when she said not to replace it, she was done. The manager came over with a whole new meal, which made the situation worse, since that wasn't what she wanted. She told the manger that the waiter needed to go back to waiter school 101 because his attitude was so bad. Needless to say, we weren't charged for the dinner.

On the other hand, even if a server somehow has a challenge with my order or the kitchen sent out the wrong order, if the attitude of the server is one of sincere apology and understanding of my frustration, he or she will still get my 20% tip.

Here's a bonus about attitude: IT'S RECESSION PROOF! You can have an attitude of gratitude every single day no matter what others say or no matter what your circumstances are. You are in control of your attitude every single day because your attitude is a choice.

Eleanor Roosevelt famously said "No one can make your feel inferior without your consent." I love that quote! Now, change the word 'inferior' to any other word to describe your mood: happy, sad, frustrated, angry, grateful...the list goes on and on! My point is, you are in control 100% of your attitude – so you might as well make it a good one! But, what does that look like? Think of someone you know who has a great attitude. Who are they?

_____

Now, describe them. What are they like?

_____

_____

_____

Chances are, you wrote something about them having a positive outlook, and they are willing to try new things without being discouraged. Maybe your wrote down that they are always helpful and exude happiness and joy in their work and in their life. Maybe you described them as being resilient and bouncing back from adversity and being generous without complaint. I would start to recognize people who have these traits and then hang out with them! Invite them to lunch. Ask them to mentor you. Ask them to serve on a special project with you.

The people who have negative attitudes are usually the people who are always complaining about how bad their situation is. They complain about their job, their boss their co-workers, their commute, their kids and the list goes on and on. Don't walk away from these people....RUN! Or, you may even say to them, "Today I am sitting in the front-row and want to have a great attitude. I want to do that by focusing on what's positive. Is there anything you can say that's positive?" This just may cause them enough confusion to walk away!

Along with having a front-row attitude, having a front-row sense of humor is also imperative. How's your sense of humor? Having a good sense of humor has been proven to provide various health benefits. There have been numerous books written about the positive effects a sense of humor can have on one's health and wellness. I personally know that having a hysterical laugh can help alleviate stressful situations. Actually, it may be helpful to wait until you are out of the situation before you laugh hysterically, but do laugh eventually!

I'll never forget sharing a cab in Orlando Florida with a businessman who was headed to the same resort that I was. After a few minutes, he asked what brings me to town. I said, "I'm speaking at this really big women's conference." Without missing a beat, he said, "I love big women. My sister is a big woman and all of her friends are big and they say that big women are going to take over the world!" I had to stop laughing in order to correct him, and say, "No, it's a really large women's conference." To which he replied, "Yup, I love large women!" Needless to say, when I did speak to this group of executive women and recalled that mis-understanding, we all got a good laugh!

Laughing at yourself is also a good sign of having a front-row attitude. It's easy in my profession to get very serious in front of an audience. I do take my role as a speaker very seriously, but I take myself lightly. I have to! If there were a book written on professional speaking, I've probably made lots of mistakes. I've tripped on my way to the lectern, I've spit on the overhead projector, and I've even spilled an entire glass of water all over my slides. But the funniest thing that's happened in front of an audience was during a trip to Alaska. Alaska is a beautiful majestic state. I met a woman in Fairbanks who filled me in on the sociological demographics of Alaska. She told me that there were so many men in relation to women, that the odds of finding a man were really good. Then, she told me she has lived in Alaska all her life, and she could unequivocally say, that the 'goods were odd'. So, the next day, I got ready to give my speech and I saw that the audience was all men. I thought to myself 'The odds are good, but the goods are odd!' Just as I said good morning to them, the button on my blouse popped off! Of all places for me to expose myself, it's in front of this audience who maybe hadn't seen that for awhile!

I have a ton of funny stories. In fact, I put them in my 'humor file' so I can refer to them often. It's a great way to have a positive attitude and feel better. Start keeping track of things that make you laugh. I mean milk out of the nose laughter! Put them in a special file or folder and then if you are ever down, re-read your entries. You may even get those endorphins released in your brain again from the laughter, or at the very least, you put a smile back on your face.

The latest entry in my personal Humor File is from a book I read about the nine coal miners that were trapped in a Pennsylvania mine shaft. Imagine nine hungry, tired, despondent men, trapped for a total of 77 hours underground. There situation was desperate and they all individually lost hope at some point during their ordeal. Luckily, they all survived and wrote a book entitled "Our Story – 77 hours that tested our friendship and our faith." I originally bought this book about the Quecreek miners as told to Jeff Goodell for inspiration. I love real life human drama stories of perseverance and faith. I was inspired, that's for sure. I also got an unexpected laugh that cracked me up! It came when I was reading about how the stress and strain had taken its toll on each of the miners, and at one point there was some dissention among them. They had to keep moving to higher ground to survive and some thought that maybe they should just give up. The group decided that they would do whatever it took to survive so they moved once more to higher ground. While they were moving one more time, one of the guys looked at the others and said "Any of you guys want to have sex before we die?" Now that's a front-row sense of humor!!!!!

Now that you have looked at the different areas of your life, go back to your self-assessment and make a decision. What area do you need to focus on first? What is the one area that represents a balcony seat for you? What one area looks to you like the area that you want to move up first? Focus all of your energy on that one chair of your life. You don't have to change your whole life right now. Just take it one chair at a time. Take baby steps and each day ask that question from Jana Stanfield's song... "What would I do today if I were brave?" Then, go for it!

TAMMY THURGOOD'S FRONT ROW STORY

After attending a presentation from Marilyn it got me thinking as to why not use this front-row theory in every day life. Like she said...you have nothing to lose. I attended a private David Cassidy concert that the American Payroll Association put on for their attendees. I was sitting at a table that was a back from the stage and off to the left. Here I was at a concert with a performer that I idolized in my teenage years. Out comes David...David Cassidy! The concert starts, camera in hand and I am thinking....I am way too far away! I need to get a little closer. Other people were heading up closer. Why not me? Well, off I go to get my place closer to the stage. I squatted for a little bit (that started hurting my knees) so then I just sat on the floor. I was so close to David Cassidy that I couldn't believe it. This goes on for a couple of songs. Ok, now people are standing up and getting closer to the stage. Whoa, wait for me. Up I go and stand right at the stage. David is singing and then he grabs a woman's hand over to my right and gives her a kiss. I am thinking...I want to do that. Well, he starts heading in my direction on the stage. I put my hand out and guess what? He takes my hand and gives ME a kiss! WOW! I felt like a teenager girl with a crush....all over again! More songs are sung and we are all having a wonderful time. He then starts singing his most famous song "I think I love you." What a great song! He is walking back and forth on the stage just singing and guess what? He is back by me again. Why not put my hand out there again? I did and he grabbed it again and he kissed it AGAIN! I have to say, one kiss would have been a dream come true but because I was in the front-row and put myself out there, I got two kisses. What a once in a lifetime experience that was! Unbelievable...was all I could think!

Thank you Marilyn for reminding me of my front row and the endless possibilities that it can bring!

— Tammy Thurgood, Littleton, Colorado

SCENE SIX

ACTION!

In the following pages, you will find the 6 strategies of what to do, and the one strategy to say away from, in order to get a front-row seat in life.

Act on your Vision

If you want to get a front-row seat in life, you have to take some sort of action. It doesn't have to be major action, just some action. Baby steps would work, as long as you are moving closer to your goal. A prime example is back about 15 years ago, I was speaking in Las Vegas. As a professional speaker, I spoke several times a year in Vegas, which is really the primary reason I moved here in 2004. However, before I moved here, my Las Vegas friend, Dani Maher had my travel schedule. When she realized I was arriving in her town the same day as an Earth Wind and Fire concert, she excitedly called to ask if I wanted to go with her and our friend Angela Ghilarducci. I love Earth, Wind and Fire, so I said yes without hesitation.

The day they picked me up from the airport was the same date as the concert. We went right from the airport to the MGM grand to buy up our tickets for that night. You can imagine where our seats were. Yup. They were in the nosebleed section, now of course known as the balcony. We arrived in plenty of time to climb up all the sections of the MGM grand and took our seats. I could barely see the stage, but I did make out that there were still empty seats in the front row. I thought to myself 'I really don't want to stay here; I want to be sitting in the front-row.'

Just as I was visualizing sitting down in front, Dani suggested we go to the concession stand before the show. We did, but the line was so long, I decided to take a walk. It wasn't any walk, mind you. It was THE walk. You know, that walk you have where you have everything under control. That walk of confidence and belonging. I left my girlfriends to buy snacks as I used my walk to get through all the security and ended up right next to the stage! I loved it! I approached a very good-looking young man and asked him what time the concert started, because now it looked like they were running a bit late. His answer pleasantly surprised me.

"The concert is supposed to start at 10:00, but my Uncle Phil isn't scheduled to be out on stage until 10:15."

"Uncle Phil? As in Philip Bailey the lead singer of Earth, Wind and Fire?"

He said, "Yeah, that's my uncle. Why, are you in the business?"

I told him I wasn't in the music business, but that I was a motivational speaker. He quickly asked me if I could motivate him! I started talking about the importance of getting out of your comfort zone, and setting goals, and having a vision and so on. I also told him I spoke on being more assertive and how to deal with difficult people. He was very interested in my speeches when the lights went down indicating the start of the concert. He apologized and told me he had to go take his seat, but that he wanted to continue our conversation. I asked him where his seat was, and he indicated right down in front. He asked me where my seat was and I turned him around and waved to the very top of the venue and said somewhere way up there! He asked me who I was with and when I told him my two girlfriends, he told me to wait while he went behind the curtain. Within minutes, he came back with three 'all access' badges! He told me to get my friends, sit anywhere that is vacant, and meet him back there right after the show!

I ran up to my girlfriends who quickly said "Marilyn, where have you been? These people tried to steal our seats!". That's when I took out our new badges and said "We're going to the front-row!" As we headed down to our new seats, Dani asked me how I did it...this time! I told her I just acted as if I knew where I was going which created the opportunity to get to the stage. There, I took the opportunity to get out of my comfort zone and start a conversation with a complete stranger. Within moments, I realized I had something of value to offer him (a mini-motivation session) and he reciprocated by offering me something I needed....front-row tickets!

My experience has been that most people take their seats, and when they see the view, they complain. Not only do people complain about the seats, but they then start bickering about why the seats are so bad and how they should have bought them earlier, and so on. Then, when people are really negative, they start to criticize the people that ARE down in front! They make up stuff as to why they lucked out or why they scored the good seats, pure conjecture. All I am saying is that if you don't like your seats, MOVE! At least make some sort of attempt to get a better seat in life. Don't be jealous or resentful of other people who seem to have a better seat. Just focus on your own seat, and see what you can do about improving it. Of course, trying to get through security in order to talk to someone at a concert will not always work. I tried it at an Elton John concert, and well, let's just say that I went back to my original seat. Speaking of concert seats, my niece Paige got two free tickets to see Brittney Spears, and she asked me to go with her. Apparently, her neighbor won them from a Supermarket promotion and Brittney Spears wasn't what she and her newborn had in mind as a fun night out. However, Paige was 14 and loved the thought of going to see Brittney Spears in concert.

Before we were let into the venue, the sponsors of the ticket give-away had some trivia questions for all the young concert goers. The winner would be up on stage during Brittney's rehearsal and sound check. Lo and behold, Paige won the trivia game and the spot on stage with Brittney for the rehearsal! She was so excited, that she called my brother and sister-in-law, her grandparents and cousins! Then, the sponsor director came over and apologized but Brittney's tour bus was caught in traffic, so the rehearsal was cancelled. It broke my heart to see the disappointment on Paige's face. The promotion person saw it too, and a half hour later came over to us with Brittney Spears concert paraphernalia: t-shirts, badge necklaces and posters. She told Paige that she wanted to make it up to her for not being able to meet Brittney. She asked if Paige would like to meet her back-up dancers. Paige's face lit up and of course said yes. That wasn't all...the promotions person gave her two front-row tickets to make up for missing the rehearsal! Yup! Front-row tickets! Paige and I had a great time! We were in the right place at the right time and it all worked out great. You just never know where your next front-row ticket is going to come from!

RICK JONES' FRONT-ROW STORY

You know the old saying that you can't judge a book by its cover? Well I am that book. I am a former professional football player, from the late 70's to the mid 80's. I made my living by being, well let's say assertive. But time brings about a change and it's amazing how we lose sight sometimes of who we really are. You would never think of me as shy and laid back especially if you ever saw me on a football field. Sometimes, by being shy, life will pass you by. Sometimes losing sight of who you are or who you want to be, life will pass you by. Nothing fails but a try.

Well, Miss. Sherman, I incorporated your philosophy of being in the front-row and stepping out of my comfort zone. Having been a football player, I have always been physically large. But after my career was over I become larger. I was 270 lbs. Knowing that was unhealthy and expensive, I lost 50 lbs. through prayer, hard work, and stepping out. Since I had lost the weight, I started thinking about being in the fitness business as a consultant.

Marilyn, you spoke of putting action to your vision, so I tried that recently in my hometown of Birmingham, Alabama. Former NBA great Charles Barkley was in Birmingham in early April for a book signing. I decided, why not meet him and express my interest in becoming his trainer or consultant? To make a long story short, I stepped right out of my comfort zone and introduced myself to Charles

Barkley. I was in the front-row meeting him, and I also had a great time meeting his mother, and his agent. He told me when I start my business to drop him a line. I was blown away by his friendliness and warmth!

What you preach in your speech about stepping out and being in the front-row and about how good things are at our fingertips is true. All we have to do is just grasp them. Take chances! After all, all you have to lose is nothing. The world turns whether we play or not. Get in the game!

- Rick Jones, Birmingham Alabama

P.S. The saying for me
(and I try to work on this everyday) is
"Courageous Confrontation". RJ.

SCENE SEVEN

INVEST IN
YOURSELF

What does it mean to invest in yourself and why is that important relating to this book? Because if you aspire to be more, have more, and to be able to give more, you really have to make those opportunities happen. Please don't wait around for a V.P. to hand you a job. Don't wait for someone to discover you and don't wait around for a front-row seat. Let's face it, some of the best seats in the house are going to cost some major bucks. However, if what you want to do, be or have is in alignment with what you truly value, then it's worth it. You're worth it. I remember asking my boss if I could go to a motivation ralley to see such greats as Zig Ziglar and Brian Tracy. It was $99.00 and as a trainer in Human Resources; I saw it as a fit for my job. My boss didn't share my vision and said no. I offered to split the cost, pay the whole cost, get the day off, and finally with my supreme negotiating skills, I agreed to pay for it myself, take my own car, and take a vacation day to go.

I am so grateful that I persisted in going to this event because I was able to meet, in person, the two great speakers I had spent years listening to on tape (yes, back in the day, I listened to audio cassette albums – this was way before downloadable podcasts). Once I met them in person, I was able to keep in touch with them and acknowledge how influential they were on my career. Brian Tracy ended up endorsing my first book and I see Zig Ziglar from time to time at our National Speakers Association conventions. In fact in 1994. I was living in San Diego and had another opportunity to invest in my personal and professional development. I owned my own company now, so I didn't need to ask permission from anyone to go. The lineup was incredible! Zig Ziglar was headlining and there were a host of other famous speakers as well including Dan Fouts, Debbie Fields, and Mary Lou Retton. The cost was only $49.00 for the full day. Then, I read the fine print. I saw that for an extra $200.00 I could have breakfast with Zig! Now I got excited. You may think $200.00 is a lot of money to have breakfast, and it certainly is. However, the chance to meet Zig and spend some quality time with him was worth it. He represents the epitome of a motivational speaker and this was my time to rub elbows with greatness. I immediately registered and then called my sister Margie. I usually don't tell her all about the various speaking conferences and conventions that I go to, but one name on this particular line up prompted me to call her. Debbie Fields. You see, my sister Margie is an avid baker. She is married with four kids and when she gets the chance, she bakes fantastic cakes and cookies. So I thought I would impress her with the fact that I was going to see Debbie Fields, who is of course famous for the Mrs. Fields' Chocolate Chip Cookies. I did get a reaction from my sister, but it wasn't the reaction that I thought. She said, "Will you do me a favor? When you see her, ask her what her secret is to her chocolate chip cookie recipe. I've read her book and tried her recipe, but mine just don't taste the same as when I buy them in the mall."

Now, I am thinking, there are going to be 10,000 people gathered at the San Diego Convention Center, how am I going to possibly even see her? I told my sister that I would do what I could, but I really didn't think it was possible. Little did I know what I had in store that day!

I showed up and was very excited to go meet Zig for breakfast. When

I went to sign in, they saw that I had purchased the VIP ticket, so I was instructed to go where the breakfast was, and then my pass would get to the roped off section in the front of the convention. I was pleasantly surprised to see Zig welcome all 200 of us who purchased the extra ticket. 200 people sounds like a lot, but compared to the 10,000 people that were going to be gathered in the main hall, 200 was a pretty intimate audience. In fact, Zig stood at the door way and welcomed each of us. I had a chance to briefly chat with him and tell him that I too was a speaker and he gave me encouraging words. I also had my picture taken with him and I was thrilled! The convention hadn't even started yet and already my investment had paid off.

After Zig gave us our own motivational talk, we all were invited to go down in the front to sit in the VIP section. I was very excited to see that our section was the first 20 rows in the middle! Therefore, I sat in the front-row, next to a reserved seat. Then, right before the opening session started, this woman came from behind the stage and sat in the reserved seat. Much to my delight, it was Debbie Fields! She was so nice. She was chatting with those of us who were close to her and she mentioned that she wasn't speaking until the afternoon, but that she wanted to hear all of the other speakers.

In between each of the speakers, there was a 15-minute intermission. So, after about the 3rd intermission, I finally mustered up the courage to say, "Hey Debbie, My sister Margie wanted me to ask you.....what's your secret to your chocolate chip cookies?" She was very nice and told me without hesitation, that it's all in the vanilla. Most people use imitation vanilla, but she suggested I tell my sister to splurge on the best vanilla she could buy!" Isn't that great? Now imagine that call to my sister. It was so funny! "Hey Margie, Debbie Field's told me to tell you to get better vanilla!" This was such a front-row moment, a front-row experience. And, it never would have happened had I not invested in myself. I like to say that once you invest in yourself to get that front-row seat; you have a greater likelihood of experiencing extra bonus front-row moments that you wouldn't have otherwise had.

A few years ago, I invested in a consultant to help me with my speaking business. My goal is to speak at 100 events a year and I needed someone to help me strategize to get there. Yves and I met him, told him all about us so he could prepare for my day of consulting. When we arrived at his office, I was prepared to talk about my business and what I was currently doing vs. what I wanted to do. I knew that we invested a lot of money for this day of consulting and I didn't want to waste a second of it! Therefore, you can imagine my surprise when he started off talking to Yves directly. I was getting a bit impatient until the idea of new business started to materialize.

He said; "Yves, you are an authentic French Baron. You used to be in the wine business and your family and friends in France are still in it. Why don't you teach people what you know? Why don't you do webinars or seminars on how to be more confident in the world of wine?"

Yves then said; "I used to host groups of Americans in France, so I could do that too!" After this day of consulting, not only did I get some direction on how to build my speaking business, but we started a new business called The Baron of Wine, Inc. Yves just published a book called 'Choosing Wine Made Easy' and we are starting to take reservations on the ultimate wine fantasy experience to France. Each fall and spring we will be taking small groups of people on exclusive 7 day excursions that include wine tastings, visits to chateaus, meeting other French nobility throughout Bordeaux, Burgundy, and Paris, and fun, fun, fun! People will learn how to order, serve, and entertain with wine not to mention having bragging rights when they come back. Can you imagine? None of this new, front-row business would have happened had we not invested in the business consultant to help me grow my business.

So, if you find an opportunity to invest in a coach, attend an event, or do something spectacular, as long as it is in alignment with your goals and your value system, yet it costs you a bit of money, then go for it! You are worth the investment! By the way, if you want to come with us to France, check out Yves' new website at www.TheUltimateWineTrip.com.

What investment could you make today to get you closer to the front-row? _____

_____

_____

What goals could you accomplish if you made the above investment?

_____

_____

If you were to invest in your personal development, what more could you accomplish? _____

_____

_____

If you are challenged financially right now, don't be discouraged. There are other ways to get to the front-row without dishing out the big bucks. Stay tuned for the next chapter to learn how you can do that.

DeBorah Little's Front-Row Story

It's amazing how faith, courage, and perseverance, can sustain you and change your life. In early 2001 I was working with a non-profit organization helping non custodial parents get off of welfare and back into the work force. It was a gratifying job in the purpose it served, but certainly not a career position for me. While surfing the Welfare to Work web site one day, I found a Welfare to Work Conference that was being held in New York City. My employer was hesitant to send me because of budget restraints, so I offered to share in the expenses so I could attend. After some negotiations, my employer agreed. I would pay for my transportation and meals and my employer would pay the conference registration fees and for my hotel. There was something about this conference that was pulling at me and I was determined to attend. I thought it was because of the information and connections it would afford me in my position. Little did I know, it would pay off larger than I could have ever imagined.

I arrived at the conference eager to meet people with a passion for helping others and working to make a difference in the lives of those less fortunate than us. I was like a sponge, soaking up the information and seeking out success stories. On the last day of the Conference, I was approached by a United Airlines Human Resources representative who offered me her card and invited me to apply for a management position with her company. I couldn't believe it! She and I had become friendly during the conference, and she shared with me that she was so impressed with me, my passion for the work I was doing, and my professionalism, that she wanted me to join her company and would do everything she could to get me onboard. What she didn't know, is that I had been praying for the past year and a half for this very type of opportunity!

It is my opinion, and my experience, that by holding onto my dreams, maintaining my faith, and persevering in the things I was passionate about, no matter what the cost, my dreams were destined to come true. I believed it with my entire being. The United Airlines Representative remains a close friend to this day. Two months after meeting her, I accepted a Management position with United Airlines in San Francisco, CA and have been living my life "In The Front Row" ever since! I married the man of my dreams, I have traveled the world and continue to do so, often taking my mother with me to Paris, Rio De Janeiro, Hawaii and other fascinating cities and every day I say a prayer of "Thanks" for the blessings in my life and the 'Front Row' life I live.

-DeBorah Little, Seattle Washington

On a personal note, success runs in DeBorah's family. She is a success in her own right, but is also married to former player #44 from the Denver Broncos, Floyd Little. What a front-row experience it was to be with DeBorah and Floyd to see him be inducted to the National Football League Hall of Fame. We are so proud of him and of his accomplishments on and off the field!

SCENE EIGHT

BE OF SERVICE

The theme of service is an obvious one. The more you give, the more you receive. Or another popular saying is "what goes around comes around." However, I am putting this in my book for a reason that is not so obvious. In fact, I don't want you to think my message is "Hey everyone, go out and give service so that you can receive something in return". Even though that is true and I do believe in the law of reciprocity, that is not why it's here. Earlier in this book, I talked about investing in yourself. If you find a front-row seat that represents alignment with your value system, then it's worth it, go for it and spend some money. But, what if you're tight on funds? What if you just can't afford to sit in the front-row? I believe there is an alternative. My message here is *don't allow lack of funds to keep you from getting a front-row seat. There is always another way!*

For example, giving service. What can you do for someone else? What burden can you lighten for someone else? What service can you provide that could be exchanged for a front-row seat? I came across this by accident, actually. I am a proud member of the National Speakers Association (NSA). Every year, we have a convention of speakers, authors, consultants, and entertainers who gather to network, learn how to grow our speaking business and reconnect with our speaker buddies. My favorite part of going is the general sessions. I always study ahead of time the schedule and find out what time the doors will open to the main ballroom. Then, I camp out. I want to be one of the first one's in there in order to grab a good seat. Often the front rows are already reserved for board members, staff, or the convention team.

I even warn people who are gathered with me waiting for the doors to open. I let them know ahead of time, that I don't mean to be rude, but when the doors open, we may be in the middle of a conversation, but I will be dashing into the ballroom to get a seat. Then, let's find each other to finish our conversation! They usually say they were going to do the same thing, and to forgive them if I was in the middle of a sentence and they bolt for the seats!

One year, I noticed the NSA staff was putting out handouts to every chair in the room. I felt silly just standing there waiting for the go ahead to enter when I offered to help them. I was just waiting after all. They appreciated my help so much that they offered me a reserved seat as a thank you! It didn't take me long to figure out that the more I offered my service the more likely I would have a front-row seat! So I volunteered for everything! I was the photographer one year, I was on the hospitality committee another year, and I was even the chair of the people movers! Then, one day I was offered the position of *General Session Speaker Concierge!* What a great title. That meant that I was assigned to all of the speakers who would be on the main stage. I was in charge of getting them to rehearsal on time, getting all of their audiovisual needs met, and basically doing anything I could to help them give a great presentation. The best part for me was getting to hang out back stage before and after their speeches. I got to know them as performers, speakers, and eventually friends. One speaker and entertainer that became my friend was Roy Firestone. Critically acclaimed for his work in broadcast journalism, Roy has won six Emmy® Awards and two Cable ACE Awards. He has interviewed more than three thousand people, including nearly every major sports figure plus an eclectic mix including former president Richard Nixon; legendary actor James Stewart; jazz great Miles Davis; comedian Jerry Lewis; and pop icon Madonna. Roy is an accomplished singer, impressionist, and humorist has shared the bill with notables such as Frank Sinatra, Loretta Lynn, Vic Damone, Gladys Knight, the Four Tops, and Frankie Valli. Appearances include Late Night with David Letterman, Later with Bob Costas, The Arsenio Hall Show, Nightline, Larry King Live, and Married with Children.

I had the great opportunity to be responsible for going in the limo to meet him at the airport and get him to the hotel, checked in, fed, and on to rehearsal. When I met Roy, he was as nice as could be. He immediately asked me about what I spoke on and how was my business going. You would never know he was a celebrity by how nice and down to earth he was. His show was fantastic by the way. I had no idea he could sing! I am a huge sports fan, so to see the great clips of sports moments, and hearing him sing, and do impersonations was so entertaining. I must have expressed my enthusiasm for his work when he was done, because he invited me to see his show whenever he was performing in my city (at the time was San Diego). Less than a year later, he was performing for the San Diego Chargers annual 'Chargers Champions' gala to raise money for local scholarships. Being Roy's guest was great. I met the owners of the Chargers, Junior Seau, and eventually sat at a great table. There were a couple of sportscasters, Marcellus Willey, Roy and on the other side of me was Doug Flutie. We had a great dinner, fabulous atmosphere and then they started the program. Marcellus spoke for a few minutes about growing up in the projects and then going to an Ivy League school and then the NFL. Then, Doug Flutie was to talk. But, before they introduced

Doug to the stage, they showed a montage of film clips hi-lighting Doug's football career. Included in this footage was his famous Hail Mary pass for Boston College to win the game over Miami to get to the national championship game. Watching the film and then watching Doug sitting next to me was surreal to say the least. Doug leaned over and said "I can't believe they still show that clip!" So I leaned over to Roy and said "I'll never get tired of seeing that clip!" I noticed Roy wasn't nearly as excited and said "'I'm tired of it...I'm from Miami!" We had a really good laugh at that one. Before the evening was over, I told Doug I was writing a book about getting a front-row seat in life and sitting next to him was indeed a front-row seat.

The following year at NSA, I was asked to be the general session concierge again and this time the line up included Stedman Graham. He is known for being a savvy business man, consultant and speaker, as well as being Oprah Winfrey's significant other. Right after I found out who was in the line-up, I got a speaking opportunity in Chicago. I arranged to stay a day later and got tickets to see a taping of the Oprah show. It was easier than I thought to get tickets. All I did was call the studio. It took a couple of days before I could get through, but I did and secured two tickets. There is no charge for tickets to Oprah's show and every seat in Harpo studios is a front-row seat.

The show that I saw was called "Women who Rock". The guests were Bonnie Raitt, KT Oslin, and Natalie Cole. Each performer sang 2 songs, gave an interview, and then left the studio. So by the time Natalie was singing, Bonnie and KT had left. I knew that Oprah talks to the audience while the cameras keep rolling for a segment on the Oxygen channel called "After the Show". She also posts the clips on her website. Since each artist left the building, I knew there was no subject for the After the Show segment, which meant an open forum. I knew I wanted to connect with Oprah, but I didn't want to sound common. I had a feeling people would say how much they loved her, how excited they were to be there, and how they rode 17 hours on a bus just to be there in person. I am sure she hears that all the time. I thought of what I could say that was unique. So, when the time was appropriate, I got her attention and she addressed me. I stood up and said:

"I'm a professional speaker and Stedman is speaking at our annual convention. I am his concierge on-site, what do you recommend I have for him in the green room?"

The audience laughed but she actually had an answer. She told me he loves oatmeal raisin cookies and don't forget the raisins. She asked me when it was, I told her and invited her to Orlando. She declined, but it was very cool to have a dialogue with Oprah. I e-mailed a friend of mine who owns Great Harvest Bread Company. I told him to check out the clip I have of me talking to Oprah on my website and does Great Harvest make oatmeal raisin cookies?

When he saw my e-mail, he couldn't figure out the connection between Oprah and his company until he saw the clip.

The night Stedman arrived at our convention, I had my own surprise. I had 5 dozen oatmeal raisin cookies that were fed-ex'd to my room. 2 ½ dozen for me and 2 ½ dozen for Stedman! (That's actually how they were labeled!) When Stedman arrived, I made sure he was all checked in and then I called room service to send him up some cold milk to go with his cookies. The next morning when I saw Stedman at rehearsal, I asked him if he got his package and he said "I LOVE oatmeal raisin cookies". I just smiled and said "That's great."

This was another front-row experience that all stemmed from a willingness to give service. How much did all of this cost me? A small fee for room service to deliver milk to Stedman's room, and that was it.

When you give service, good things do happen. The spirit of giving is so rich. I love the quote that says you cannot light the wick of someone else's candle without it growing your flame at the same time. Again, I am not saying that is why we give service. But, isn't it nice to know that there's still a way to get to the front-row when we are short on funds? That is encouraging!

What talent, act, or resource can you provide in the spirit of service?

_____

_____

What can you do to help someone else, and ease his or her burden, no matter how small?

_____

_____

BILL STAINTON'S FRONT-ROW STORY

"What's your value?" As a humorist, I get asked that question a lot. (Fortunately, it's never happened after a presentation...yet!) Like you, I have my stock answers, and, to the extent that meeting planners hire me, they're effective. But if I were to be honest, I'd have to admit that I sometimes ask that question of myself. And I know, from conversations I've had with some of you, that you do too. When I'm working as a humorist (as opposed to my more "content" driven programs) I don't teach people how to increase sales, or how to lead more effectively, or how to invest more wisely. I just make them laugh. And really, shouldn't I be doing something more important? What, indeed, is the value?

I used to be the producer of a hit comedy TV show in Seattle. We were number one in our time slot for ten straight years, and when we finally left air, it was front page news for two days in a row. Despite the show's success, I sometimes found myself asking, "Shouldn't I be doing something more important?"

And then I got the letter.

It was from a woman—a viewer—whose name I no longer remember. But her son's name was Jeff. Jeff was seventeen years old, and was dying of cancer. It turns out he was a fan of the show, and his birthday was coming up. Jeff's mom was hoping we could send him an autographed photo of the cast. Instead, we decided to throw Jeff a party. I called Jeff's mom, told her our plan, and asked her if it should be a surprise or not. She told me that a surprise would probably be too much for Jeff to handle, and that she'd let him know.

So we ordered a cake, autographed several pictures, and drove to Seattle's Children's Hospital. A few of Jeff's hospital friends were there, and some nurses and doctors stopped by. I doubt if we were there longer than two hours.

Two weeks later, I got the second letter. Jeff had died a week after his eighteenth birthday. But there was no self-pity in the letter. Instead, Jeff's mom was thankful. She said that she hadn't seen Jeff as happy in nearly a year as he was on the day of his party. She literally couldn't remember the last time she had seen him laugh…but he laughed that day.

— Bill Stainton, Seattle, Washington

* I asked Bill to write me a front-row story because I knew a bit about his background. With 29 Emmy awards, surly he has a bunch of front-row experiences. This letter was written for speakers who are humorists, and when I read it, I told Bill, 'sounds like a front-row story to me!' and he gave me permission to use it. Thanks Bill for showing us that there are many ways to give service.

CHAPTER
NINE

APPRECIATE
THE SEAT THAT
YOU'RE IN

I've often heard that you don't really appreciate what you have until you don't have it anymore. That is certainly true. A number of years ago I was having a minor melt-down at the thought of turning 40. I started the ever so dangerous thought of comparison. I was comparing where I was in life vs. where I thought I would be at 40. Then I started comparing myself to where I was in my career to people younger than me who were further along in their career. I know the comparison trap is just that: a trap. Whenever you compare yourself with anyone else, you never come out equal, you're either better or worse off. But you also have to take in consideration the whole life of the person you are comparing yourself to. Sure, they may have a better business than you, but if you look at how they compromised their family to get it, would you still be envious? Anyway, I was able to snap out of my comparison trap by the help of my good friend Dave Carothers. He has a twin brother Davey who works in Hollywood as a cameraman. Dave told me about a location shoot that Davey went on in the Bahamas. I can just imagine how beautiful this particular video shoot was and I wonder if any one of them said "I can't believe we get paid to be here. It doesn't get any better than this."

After the shoot was over, there was a group that was to take a shuttle to the airport to catch a private plane to Florida. Davey wasn't scheduled to be on that flight, but he desperately wanted to be on it. He didn't make the shuttle so he took a cab to the airport to catch up with the rest of the group. Have you ever been in hurry? Have you ever really wanted to be someplace else, and you were anxious, and frustrated and maybe a little flustered? Maybe you're not where you want to be in your work, or you aren't where you want to be physically or even socially or spiritually. Don't allow your anxiety to rule you. Maybe you can learn from Davey. You see, as the cab pulled up toward the airport, they could see the private plane take off without him. Disappointed? I'm sure Davey was pretty upset until much to their shock and amazement, they saw the plane crash! R and B star Aaliya and her crew had too much luggage and the weight of the cargo caused the plane to go down just 200 yards beyond the runway. Six people died immediately, and the remaining two died at the hospital later. Now, that was a close call for Davey.

Whenever I get anxious, or in a hurry, or start to think that I'm not in the seat that I want to be in, I think of Davey wanting that seat on the plane that crashed. Then I think, maybe I'm exactly where I am supposed to be. Maybe I need to really appreciate where I am so that when there is an opportunity for my front-row seat to be available to me, I am ready. But, it's important that you are prepared.

I remember living in Allentown working as a writer in the training department of a large finance company. My goal was to be a trainer, but I knew that I had to prove myself writing training programs first before I could present them. Knowing what my goal was, I started preparing early. I created a file at my desk that I labeled 'dream workshop'. Every time I read something, saw something, or participated in something that I thought would be good in a training session that I could present, I put it in the file. Not too long after being in this position, I was asked to participate in a video that would be used for new-hires at the company. I showed up at the designated conference room and met a few other people including a gentleman named Joe Fagan. Mr.

Fagan was the president of the commercial division of our company. I worked in the consumer division, so our paths would normally never cross. In fact, they had their own outside training resources and didn't use our services...yet.

The director of the video told us that we could talk about anything we wanted, as they were only looking for video footage and no audio. They were going to add a voice-over later. When the director said 'Action' I jumped all over it. I turned to Mr. Fagan and said;

"Mr. Fagan, it is so good to see you. I just finished writing a sales training program that I think would be great for your division. It's motivational, inspirational, content-filled, and I guarantee it will help you increase your sales. When I get back to my office, why don't I ask my secretary to send you up a copy of the outline and we can make this happen. What do you say?"

Mr. Fagan was very interested and asked me to tell him more, so I did. Eventually, the director said 'Cut – we have enough footage, you can all go.' Much to my surprise, Mr. Fagan said; "I really am interested in your program, can I see it?" I told him I would send it up later that afternoon. Then, I got busy.

I ran to my cubical (I didn't have an office) and I went to my dream workshop file and pulled out anything that had to do with sales (I didn't have a sales training program that I had written...yet). I sent it up to his office (I didn't have a secretary) and was shocked at the next call that I got. It was from his Sr. Vice President, who never would have had a reason to call me in the past. We were breaking all political lines that had been previously established. Apparently, he read my material and told me about them planning a sales meeting in Allentown and they were pulling in all the sales people from around the country. They had already hired an outside speaker, but now they wanted me to go on first and do my program.

My boss was ecstatic, because his territory immediately increased. Mr. Fagan was happy because he found an internal resource for training. I was happy, because that day, I became a speaker.

Did I know that I was going to meet Mr. Fagan that day? No. Did I know that they were going to have a sales training meeting? No. All I knew was that I had a vision and a belief that I would one day be a speaker. You never know when you will have an opportunity to move yourself closer to the front-row. You may not have a detailed plan, but have the goal and the belief in yourself and watch the plan emerge along the way. Incidentally, the sales meeting went great.

I had the honor of speaking at the National Restaurant Association (NRA) on a topic called 'Front-Row Service; How to increase your Tip Percentage and Check Average in Your Restaurant'. Before I went, I interviewed the president and CEO of NRA, Dawn Sweeney. I asked her what can people do to move up in their career. She told me something that reflected what this chapter is all about. She said to knock it out of the park in the job you have now, get noticed and see where that takes you. I love that. Yes, have your eyes on your goals, but make sure you aren't neglecting your immediate responsibilities, the seat that you are in right now.

What seat are you in now that you don't fully appreciate?

_____

_____

_____

What attitude or perspective can you shift in order to appreciate that seat?

_____

_____

_____

LOU HECKLER'S FRONT-ROW STORY

My favorite front row story:

In 1972 it was a rare father who got to see his baby being born. I was one of those dads. I was a soldier at Fort Benjamin Harrison, Indiana and the base hospital there had only a small number of births each year, so fathers were allowed to be in the delivery room.

I suited up in the blue scrubs and sat behind my wife Jonellen's head. A strategically-placed mirror allowed me to see what was happening. Truth is, we were both un-prepared: our baby was arriving six weeks early and we were Red Cross Birth Class dropouts after just one meeting as a result!

Basically I sat and tried to be comforting while Jonellen did all the work. She worked hard and worked well. Finally, the doctor held the baby up to us and declared, "We have a little boy here!" Steven Heckler...six weeks early...eleven minutes after 12 noon...April Fool's Day for gosh sakes!

I've never had a better front row seat!

- Lou Heckler, Gainesville, Florida

SCENE TEN
"DOWN IN FRONT!"

What NOT to do!

Throughout this book I've been talking about what to do to get a front-row seat in life. This chapter is all about what NOT to do. The one trait that shows you've gone too far. It's very simple and that is DON'T BE COCKY! When you are cocky, you simply repel people! Have you ever been to a reception or an event where you are mingling with people and there's always someone who is talking non-stop about how great they are and what great things they are doing? If you try to add something to the conversation, they always find a way to one-up you with a bigger story or a bigger 'get'. Cocky is basically being overconfident to the point of being arrogant. I think there is a fine line that separates being confident and being cocky. If you are confident, you know what you know and you just know it. Cocky is when you know what you know, and you have to tell every one what you know. And, you have no problem telling people what you know whether you know them or not is immaterial.

I realize that when people are cocky, and arrogant, and talking about themselves, that it could be a fear or insecurity coming out. At least that's what happened to me. I was speaking in Los Angeles to a group of mostly men, doing a program on customer service and leadership.

I had a call from a friend of mine who was in town for the Lakers game. He works for the NBA and when we are in the same city at the same time during basketball season, he gets me tickets. Well, I went to my audience with all of this excitement that I was going to see the Lakers play that night. Looking back at it now, I see that fear and or insecurity on my part led me to this behavior which actually was pretty cocky. One of the men in my audience pleaded with me to call my friend back and ask for a 2nd ticket. He figured since I knew someone, I could do that for him. I didn't know this guy very well, and now that I think of it, he was using one of my techniques about getting a front-row seat! I really didn't want to say yes, but because I had basically bragged about it so much, I didn't have the courage to politely say no. I called my friend back and he said no problem, he would get me a 2nd ticket, both of which would be under my name at will call. This participant was very excited and couldn't believe his luck! (It's great when you ask and then you receive!).

That night, I went to the Staples center and took my seat. It was about 10 rows up from the floor behind one of the baskets. Not a bad seat at all, especially since it was a gift from my friend. The whole game though, I was distracted looking over my shoulder for the arrival of my guest. And, much to my surprise, he never showed up! I couldn't believe it! After the game, I had a credential to get into the waiting area where the players and coaches come out. It was great to see my friend and to re-connect and talk about old times, including the great game we just saw. Then he asked me where my friend was. I was embarrassed to say "he didn't show up." My friend reacted in such a way, that I thought I really had done something wrong. He went on to explain that he had an empty seat next to him, right behind the Lakers bench that had my name on it. But, when I called back to get a 2nd ticket, he put me in the section that I was in figuring I would want to sit with that person! Argh! Don't you hate that? I have learned my lesson about being cocky. Now, I know that it's perfectly okay to share good news with your inner circle of friends that you know and that you mutually exchange the blessings in your life. I share my successes and pains with Lori, and also with my BFF Jill Prout. These are conversations that are private and really help bond our friendship. Otherwise, shut up. People don't like it when you boast, brag, or go on and on for the purpose of making yourself look good. Confident? Great. Cocky? Nope. Get down in front – we can't see the screen over your fat head!

Another perfect example of being cocky and how it had a terrible outcome was the 2006 Torino Winter Olympics. The event was Women's Snowboard Cross and 20-year old Lindsey Jacobellis had a few short yards until the finish line to capture gold. She knew she had won the gold – and then she got cocky. She attempted some sort of hot-dog move to showoff and when she attempted the move by grabbing her board, she crashed and slid to silver as her competitor swept by her for the gold! It was the most disappointing silver medal ever awarded! For four years she had to carry the weight of that moment on her shoulders. When she arrived in Vancouver four years later for the 2010 Winter Olympics, people said she was out for redemption. Unfortunately, she came in fifth.

Whew. I know it would be pretty hard to live down that split-second moment where she got cocky and it cost her the gold medal.

Think of a time when you acted cocky or arrogant. What was the situation?

_____

_____

_____

What will you do next time in order for you to not come across so cocky?

_____

_____

_____

ROY FIRESTONE'S FRONT-ROW STORY:

One of the great front row seat stories really is very basic: When I was 20 and on the verge of losing my job in Miami (my first television job)..the news director there was a guy who was very arrogant and mean. He kept belittling my work, my age and my talent...when he called me in to fire me, he said, in a very condescending tone... "Roy we think you belong in a smaller market."..to which I replied "Dow, there is nothing smaller than right here."

To some people that's cocky...to me it was an affirming comeback line that I never before had felt capable of because I am basically not a confrontational person.

The rest is history.

After being fired I remembered that put down as a kind of motivator for everything that ever happened to me. On national television on the "Tom Snyder" show I told that story one night and the next day I got dozens and dozens of emails and phone calls telling me that sometimes being hit makes you hit back and stand your ground. You can stand and watch as someone trashes you...or you can take out the trash, so to speak...and clean up your act...and life...That's it for me!

– Roy Firestone, Los Angeles, California

* You can see Roy play in himself in the blockbuster hit Jerry McGuire with Tom Cruise, Reneé Zellweger, Cuba Gooding Jr. and Regina King. How's that for a smaller market?!

SCENE
ELEVEN

BE PERSISTENT

Winston Churchill said in his famous speech "Never give in, never give in, never, never, never, never-in nothing, great or small, large or petty – never give in except to convictions of honor and good sense."

Over the years, people have changed his words to say that he got up and said "Never, never, never give up" and then sat back down. Either way, I like his message! There are many stories of people who demonstrated great persistence and drive to achieve their goals. Read biographies of people – this is a directive straight from my dad who is always encouraging me to read biographies of people to learn their struggles and what they did to overcome them. One of the most harrowing stories of persistence that I read about came from three Aboriginal girls from Australia in the 1930's named Molly, Daisy, and Gracie. Following an Australian government edict in 1931, black aboriginal children and children of mixed marriage were gathered up by whites and taken to settlements to be assimilated. They have called this period in Australia the "lost generation." Molly, Daisy and Gracie, were 8, 11 and 15 years old when they were taken from the arms of their grandmother, mothers and aunts and taken 800 miles away. There, they were forbidden to speak their native language as they were being schooled to be hired as domestics. Eventually they were to be bred into white society and eventually there would be no more Aborigines. These girls showed more perseverance than anyone I've ever known or read about. They escaped this camp and found what was known as the Rabbit Proof Fence that spanned 1000 miles throughout the desert toward their home. Over a month of walking, carrying each other, living off emus and feral cats, avoiding the police and trackers, they made it home. 800 miles on foot with only their perseverance, persistence, and their longing to be with their families as their fuel. Molly grew up, married, and had children of her own. Her daughter Doris Pilkington wrote a book about her mom's ordeal titled "Rabbit Proof Fence." It tells the story of the three young girls and how they defied all of the odds against them to make it home. The book was made into a movie of the same name. I recommend renting the DVD so you can see the extra footage. It's an amazing story of survival from three very smart girls. Whenever I think I'm tired, and I just can't go on, I think of little Molly carrying her younger sister who could no longer walk on her own, braving the Australian elements day and night just to walk home. Talk about being the ultimate survivor – they outwitted, outlasted, and out-survived their trackers!

Another story of persistence is the late, great Este Lauder. Her act of persistence is quite different but yielded great results. She was a young businesswoman with a passion for making women feel good. She had oils, lotions, and perfumes that she called "hope in a jar." The only problem was, she had a hard time selling to department store buyers. She wanted the bigger outlets to carry her line but she kept getting doors closed on her. One day she was in a department store in Paris and right there in the cosmetic department she was meeting the stores' buyer. Again, she was getting a 'no' from the buyer, they just weren't interested. Just then, Este Lauder dropped her bottle of perfume and it shattered on the floor. Suddenly there was all of this commotion from the customers! People were clamoring to find out what that fragrance was, and how could they get their hands on some! The buyer finally saw the popularity and the potential in carrying Este Lauder products, and immediately placed an order to sell to the excited shoppers on the spot. Este Lauder went on to build a billion dollar cosmetic empire that all started with a bit of persistence.

William Arthur Ward said, "Adversity causes some men to break; others to break records."

What adversity do you have in your life that is keeping you from getting a front-row seat? What can you do today to be persistent in moving up?

_____

_____

_____

Bea van der Voort's Front-Row Story

When my husband and I were crossing a difficult financial patch, it was my turn to help. I had never really worked before and was in my thirties. After taking 2 intensive classes I decided to start my own business and became a decorative painter. I needed a station wagon and the only one we could find was a stick shift. After a couple of hours with my husband "teaching" me, I was on my own. That Monday, work took me to "The most crooked street in the world", Lombard street in San Francisco. Terrified and alone I set out to conquer that steep city. I was nauseous with fear and anxiety but I managed to reach my client. That day, I knew I could do anything. I never turned down a job. It was my front row seat, setting me free from my fears.

– Bea van der Voort, Puerto Vallarta, Mexico

SCENE TWELVE

BE GUTSY!

Sometimes, ya just gotta be gutsy! When you have an opportunity, just go for it! As long as it doesn't hinder or hurt anyone else, and of course it's legal, than why not? Back in 1995, Mark Victor Hanson and Jack Canfield were enjoying the success of *A Second Helping of Chicken Soup* from the popular *Chicken Soup for the Soul* series. This was the beginning of an amazing journey in the publishing world with inspirational stories of every kind. Jack Canfield the co-author, was hosting a week-long seminar for speakers, educators and facilitators. This was an incredible week of learning and growing and helping others through the study of human potential and self-esteem. During that week in Los Angeles, Jack announced that his partner Mark Victor Hanson would be speaking at a group not too far from where we were. This was going to be a breakfast meeting open to the public. A group of us that were interested met very early that morning for the 7:00 breakfast meeting. Much to our surprise, the room that held approximately 200 people in rounds of 10 were already full when we arrived! Apparently, we didn't arrive early enough, which by the way should be a strategy for getting a front-row seat. The registrar told us to go the standing room only section in the back of the ballroom. We went back there, and that area was full. She then told us that there was patio seating behind the standing room only section. We went back there and it was pitiful. I stood on my toes, and I could see Mark sitting in the center table up front, but I could barely see him. Then, they started the meeting as I thought to myself "I'm so not a patio person!" The women who introduced Mark gave such a wonderful introduction, that the audience gave him a standing ovation – before his speech! Within a split second, I made a decision that had I thought about it, I may not have done it. I clapped right along with all the other now standing people as I walked unobtrusively through the crowd, all the way to the front, and then, simply sat in Mark's seat. I figured for the next hour, he wasn't going to need it!

I had a great time, saw a great speech from the front-row, and after Mark was done, he came back to the table. Whoops, the meeting wasn't over! So, I just scooted to the next open seat that was now vacant by another speaker. Mark and I have become friends and he was kind enough to endorse this book. Mark and Jack both are definitely front-row people. With all of their work in speaking and compiling incredible stories for their Chicken Soup series they are helping others be front-row people too. In fact, I would even label them as ushers. What are ushers after all? They are the people who look at your ticket stub and lead you to your seat. They guide you and give you the most direct route. They are helpful with tools like knowledge of the venue, and light to lead you when the lights are already down. Mark and Jack are like that. They have so much success between them, that they are constantly helping other people move up to their own front-rows. They are ushers, guiding the way for people to move up.

What are you doing to be an usher for someone else? Marianne Williamson said, "Success means we go to sleep at night knowing that our talents and abilities were used in a way that served others." You have talents, you have knowledge, you have access. Who do you know that needs a little direction? Who do you know that needs a little boost? Now that you are almost done reading this book, start to think of ways that you can help someone who needs a little bit of help. Make a note of people you know who you could help get closer to their front-row seat. How? Maybe it's a phone call, a note, or a visit. What can you do to make someone's day? Grab a flashlight, match, candle or a spotlight and help usher someone to their front-row seat. I encourage you to do that. In fact, today is the day!

I would like to share with you a poem that I wrote called "Today is the Day." I was 17 and obviously had positive role models growing up. My parents were my role models and I had influential teachers, administrators, and coaches at Mercer Island High School as well. I was also moved by a speaker named Roger Crawford who spoke to our class. After seeing him speak, I wrote this poem and decided that I too, wanted to become a speaker. I also wanted to be the youngest author on the Phil Donohue show, that never happened, but that's okay. It's been 30 years since I wrote this, and it's just as meaningful today. When I speak on "Whose Comfort Zone Are You In?" I end with this poem. Many of my participants have asked for a copy of it, so I share it with you on the following page. Feel free to make your own copies if you wish to share it with others.

TODAY IS THE DAY

Don't be afraid, to let people see
The warmth deep within you
Willing to be Free.
For if you take the chance,
to share that special part of you
Someone will detect it
And share their special gift too.
When you're feeling good
Anyone would know…
Your smile, your eyes, it would certainly show
You are special; special indeed
You can blossom
You can grow
You already have the seed
The most important part,
is to know that you're okay
When you feel that
You are definitely on your way.
Today you can begin
For tomorrow is too far
Today is the day
To enjoy who you are!

– Marilyn Sherman
Written in 1980

EPILOGUE

Congratulations! Now, you've done it. You are done reading this book and it's time to take some action! Today is the day to help yourself, to help others, to be a front-row person. When you start to get your own front-row seats, which I know you will, please keep me posted. I've even added a blank page at the end of this book with a simple title: Front-Row Stories. That's for you to start collecting your stories, your journey to the front-row. I love hearing front-row success stories. Simply write me at <u>Marilyn@Marilynsherman.com</u> and put "Front-Row Story" in the subject line. I might even publish it in my next version of this book!

By the way, I started this book with a dedication to my niece Haley Schroeder. A couple of years ago, when I was thinking of the concept of this book, I had been talking to my sister Margie about it. We were sitting around the fire pit in their backyard watching the 4th of July fireworks. Haley was in my lap and asked me about this new book. I think she thought it was a children's book! So, I was stumbling to articulate to my nine year old niece that she didn't have to settle for any balcony seat in life. I wanted to tell her that she was a precious child and that she deserved all the great things that life has to offer, right in the front-row. She didn't have to settle for bad relationships, work that didn't honor her, situations that were general admission. She deserved to sit in the front-row of her life and her whole life of opportunity was in front of her! But, she interrupted me before I got that far. She enthusiastically looked up to me and said, "Aunt Marilyn,

I'm in the front-row right now." It was a special moment for sure. In one sentence, she communicated to me what I was struggling to say. Naturally, when I asked her if I could use this very story, she said yes. Then when I asked her where to put it, she with your own front-row philosophy said, "Put it at the beginning, and dedicate it me too!" How does a 9-year old know about book dedications anyway? Well, Miss Haley, you can see, I did put you in the beginning with a special dedication, and I am ending with you too. Here's to your front-row seat!

About Marilyn Sherman

M arilyn loves to sit in the front-row. She is so excited about getting a front-row seat in life, she has now written the book on it. She also is a professional speaker inspiring audiences of all kinds to get a front-row seat in life. She has been speaking professionally since 1993 and is the author of another motivational book titled "Whose Comfort Zone Are You In? How to lead the life you want and be happy every day!" She also authored a motivational companion journal called "My Ticket to the Front-Row – A 52 week journal of inspiration to guide you to the Front-Row."

Marilyn is a member of the National Speakers Association and has served on a national and local committees. When not being in the front-row by speaking to audiences of every kind, Marilyn enjoys going to France with Yves – especially with friends on his ultimate wine fantasy experience!

Book Marilyn Sherman
To Speak At Your Next Event!

Marilyn Sherman, professional speaker and author, is uniquely qualified to speak to the hearts and minds of your audience members. Her presentations are ideal for those meetings and events where inspiration is the order of the day. Book her for a keynote and a bonus workshop where she can facilitate the growth process and make a real difference for your people.

She speaks to audiences of all types and sizes. Your people will never forget her infectious smile, hearty laugh, and her sparkle on stage as she shares her walk and her talk about gaining clarity, focus, and adapting a positive attitude and outlook on life. Her keynotes are titled "Why Settle for the Balcony? How to get a Front-Row Seat in Life", and "Whose Comfort Zone Are You In? How to lead the life and be happy every day!" She also conducts workshops on "Communicating for Results: From Conflict to Cooperation."

For availability, call Call Sarah Whitten at 913-498-9775 or go to her website at www.MarilynSherman.com. Her speaking schedule is updated daily so you can see where she is. And, if she is scheduled to speak in a city near you, call today to book an additional program at a discounted rate. You can watch Marilyn in action by viewing her demo video there as well. And, if you are in the foodservice industry, please visit www.FoodserviceFanatic.com. Thanks so much and we'll see you in the front-row!

CONCESSION STAND!

Motivational Resources
by Marilyn Sherman

Motivational Books by Marilyn Sherman	# of items	Price
"Whose Comfort Zone Are You In? How to lead the life you want and be happy every day!	_____	$14.95
"My Ticket to the Front-Row; A 52 week journal w/inspiration to guide you to the front-row!	_____	$14.95
"Why Settle for the Balcony? How to Get a Front-Row Seat in life!"	_____	$14.95
"Front Row Service; How to Increase Tip Percentage and Check Average"	_____	$20.00

DVD's

*Success Strategies that Work. How to create a
vision, set goals and lead an extraordinary life.* _____ $77.00

*Communication Skills that Work. How to
resolve conflict and increase cooperation.* _____ $77.00

Inspired Leadership _____ $77.00

Other resources

*Choosing Wine Made Easy; 47 tips to help you
be more confident in the world of Wine. Written by
Yves de Boisredon, The Baron of Wine* _____ $20.00

Success Outside Your Comfort Zone: On-Line 2 minute a day video
messages of hope and inspiration delivered to your smart phone or
email. This 6 week program can be bulk purchased. Please call for
details.

Individual purchase: _____ $49.95

Shipping and handling:

1 item $3.00 _____

2 items $4.00 _____

3 or more $5.00 _____

Total # items to be shipped: _____ **Total Cost: $**_____

**Please go to Marilyn's website for more motivational
resources. www.MarilynSherman.com**

Please indicate method of payment:

❑ Check made out to: "UpFront Presentations"

❑ Discover ❑ MasterCard ❑ Visa ❑ AMX

Complete information below and Mail to:

UpFront Presentations at 9030 W. Sahara Ave #444, Las Vegas, NV 89117

Today's Date: ____/____/____ Phone # (___) ____ - _____

Credit Card Number: _____

Exp. Date: ____/____

Signature:_____

Print Name:_____

Title:_____Company: _____

Address:_____

City: _____State: _____ Zip: _____

Fax: _____E-Mail: _____

Thank you so much for your order! Have a great day, and I'll see YOU in the front-row

Front-Row Stories: